S0-BZQ-837

Oakland (CA) Public Library
Elmhurst Branch
J 297.362 ANDERSON
Anderson, Sheila
Ramadan
32141040221115   06/11/2015

Ramadan

by Sheila Anderson
illustrated by Holli Conger

Content Consultant: Dr. Pamela R. Frese
Professor of Anthropology, College of Wooster

magic wagon

visit us at www.abdopublishing.com

Published by Magic Wagon, a division of the ABDO Group, 8000 West 78th Street, Edina, Minnesota 55439. Copyright © 2010 by Abdo Consulting Group, Inc. International copyrights reserved in all countries. All rights reserved. No part of this book may be reproduced in any form without written permission from the publisher.

Looking Glass Library™ is a trademark and logo of Magic Wagon.

Printed in the United States.

Text by Sheila Anderson
Illustrations by Holli Conger
Edited by Mari Kesselring
Interior layout and design by Becky Daum
Cover design by Becky Daum
Special thanks to cultural consultant Dr. Khaleel Mohammed, Department of Religious Studies, San Diego State University

Library of Congress Cataloging-in-Publication Data
Anderson, Sheila.
  Ramadan / by Sheila Anderson ; illustrated by Holli Conger.
     p. cm. — (Cultural holidays)
  ISBN 978-1-60270-605-7
  1. Ramadan—Juvenile literature. 2. Fasts and feasts—Islam—Juvenile literature. I. Conger, Holli. II. Title.
  BP186.4.A63 2010
  297.3'62—dc22
                              2008050566

Table of Contents

What Is Ramadan?

Ramadan is the Muslim holy month of fasting. Muslims are people who follow the Islamic faith. Muslims live all over the world.

During Ramadan, Muslims do not eat or drink throughout the day. They eat before the sun rises in the morning. They eat again after the sun has set at night.

What does it mean to fast? Fasting is when people choose not to eat or drink. During Ramadan, healthy people fast during daylight hours for the whole month.

Some people do not fast during Ramadan.
People who are old, sick, or pregnant do not fast.
Children do not have to fast until they are about
12 years old. Some younger children do try to
fast. They may fast for only part of the day or
a few days of the month.

Ramadan's Story

Muhammad is the founder of Islam. Muslims believe God told Muhammad how people should live their lives. Muhammad repeated the messages from God aloud to people who would listen. These messages were later written down in the Muslim holy book. This book is called the Quran.

Islam is the world's second-largest religion. More than 1 billion Muslims practice Islam throughout the world.

Ramadan is an Arabic word. It means "hot month." Muhammad heard the messages from God in the summer. The weather was hot. Muslims believe God talked to Muhammad during the month of Ramadan. It has been a special month ever since then.

Ramadan does not always come in the summer. The Muslim calendar is a lunar calendar. This means it follows the moon's cycles. The calendar used in the United States is a solar calendar. This means it is based on the number of days it takes Earth to travel around the sun.

Ramadan falls in the ninth month of the lunar calendar. It can happen in winter, spring, summer, or fall.

A Day During Ramadan

The Ramadan fast begins the day of the new moon. During Ramadan, families eat breakfast early in the morning. They must eat before the sun rises. This morning meal is called the *suhoor*. After suhoor, they say a special prayer. They will not eat or drink again until the sun sets that night.

In the evening, people wait for the moon to be seen. Then, they can eat and drink again. Before eating supper, many Muslims break their fast by drinking water and eating a few dates. After this, families pray together.

20

After the sunset prayer, people gather for supper with family and friends. This is the evening meal. It is called the *iftar*.

Many restaurants close during daylight for Ramadan. They reopen for iftar. They may have special foods. Sometimes large tents are set up outside restaurants. This way, many people can eat together. Ramadan is a joyous month of gathering.

The Muslim place of worship is called a mosque. Muslim men and women do not worship together in mosques. They worship in separate areas.

Fasting and Praying

Muslims fast during Ramadan so they can think only about God. They give God their full attention instead of thinking about food.

Muslims also fast so they are reminded of those who are suffering. They think of people who do not have enough to eat. They learn to be thankful for what they have. During Ramadan, it is also a tradition for people to give to the poor. They give money or food. This is called *Zakaat*.

Muslims who are unable to fast must make up for not fasting. They must try to fast the same number of days during another time of the year. If they still cannot fast, they may feed a poor person the same number of days that they were unable to fast.

During Ramadan, Muslims try not to fight, lie, or be mean to others. People work on being kind and caring. They try to be better people and live peaceful lives.

Muslims pray five times a day throughout the year. During Ramadan, Muslims pray even more often. They also spend more time studying the Quran. Some families try to read the whole Quran during Ramadan. At the mosque, they may read one part of the Quran each night. By the end of the month, they will have read the whole book.

The Night of Power is a special night during Ramadan. On this night it is believed Muhammad heard the first verse of the Quran from God. To celebrate this special night, many Muslims pray at the mosque all night long.

Celebrations Today

Ramadan ends at the next new moon. For three days after the end of Ramadan, Muslims celebrate Eid al-Fitr. These are feasting days. People celebrate the end of the fast. It is an exciting time.

On the first day of Eid al-Fitr, everyone bathes. They put on new clothes. They go to the mosque for special prayers. They also give money or food to the poor.

During Eid al-Fitr, women may paint patterns on their hands with a paint called henna. Men often get haircuts.

People travel to be with family and friends for Eid al-Fitr. They give each other cards and gifts. Some families have parties and share big meals. They might enjoy a treat called baklava for dessert. They are thankful for all the good things they have.

Glossary

dates—a dried fruit.

holy—belonging to God.

Islam—a religion in which the followers believe in one God and study the Quran.

prayer—a communication with God.

tradition—customs, ideas, and beliefs handed down from one generation to the next.

On the Web

To learn more about Ramadan, visit ABDO Group online at **www.abdopublishing.com**. Web sites about Ramadan are featured on our Book Links page. These links are routinely monitored and updated to provide the most current information available.

Index